A Book For Lovers Of Parties And Delicious Drinks

TABLE OF CONTENTS

DESIGNATION

-M- ;   recipes requiring a mixer
-S- ;   recipes requiring a shaker
-W- ;   recipes for which a mixer and
          shaker are not necessary

* Rate the taste of the drink on a scale of 1-5 stars *

GENERAL LIST OF ITEMS AND INGREDIENTS

ALCOHOL:

- gin
- dark rum
- white rum
- tequila silver
- whisky
- sparkling wine/champagne

- liqueur : mint, Blue Curacao, mint, strawberry, chocolate, cherry (I recommend Italian) cream (definitely Irish), peach (I recommend English), herb and spice (German is perfect), coconut (coconut-rum), coffee (Mexican is delicious), almond (I recommend Italian) triple sec liqueur..,

- vodka
- black vodka
- flavored vodka: currant, passion fruit, watermelon, orange,

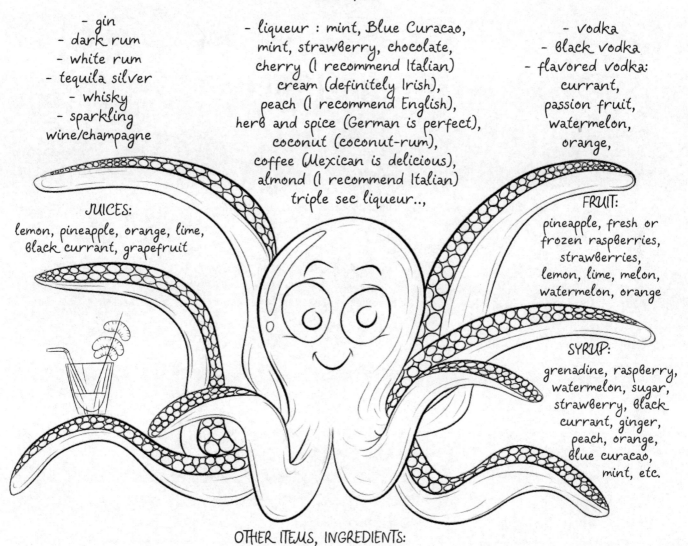

JUICES:

lemon, pineapple, orange, lime, black currant, grapefruit

FRUIT:

pineapple, fresh or frozen raspberries, strawberries, lemon, lime, melon, watermelon, orange

SYRUP:

grenadine, raspberry, watermelon, sugar, strawberry, black currant, ginger, peach, orange, blue curacao, mint, etc.

OTHER ITEMS, INGREDIENTS:

- Low/high glasses
- Ice trays
- Spoon (I recommend a bartender's spoon with a muddler)
- Paper straws
- Double sided measuring cup
- Shaker (if you don't have one, a jar will do)
- Citrus squeezer
- Blender/Mixer

Tabasco sauce, Coffee creamer/milk, condensed sweetened & unsweetened milk, mint leaves, ice cubes, canned coconut milk, tonic, sparkling water, gingerbread spice, Sparkling lemon-lime soda, brown sugar, Cinnamon stick for garnish, Bitters.

HELPFUL TIPS

Crushed ice

Instead of using an ice crusher, you can do it another way.
For example, by wrapping the ice in a cloth and
pounding it with a meat mallet.

A few drops

The easiest way to do this is with a straw – I use my finger
to plug the straw on one side, and dip it into the syrup on
the other side, then move it over the shot glass and "tap" the
straw, the contents will flow into the glass.

RASPBERRY PINA COLADA
-M-

Just perfect for hot days. It is a sweet drink that
tastes delicious, tropical, and refreshing.
It goes perfectly with fresh raspberries but frozen
raspberries are just as good.

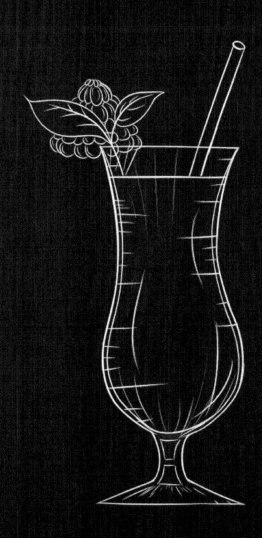

Raspberry Pina Colada

Preparation time: 15 min
Serves: 1

Ingredients:

- 40 ml of white rum
- 40 ml of canned coconut milk
- 3 slices of pineapple
- a handful of frozen raspberries
- crushed ice
- Pineapple slice for garnish

Instructions:

Mix all ingredients in a blender and pour into a glass. Decorate with pineapple.

STRAWBERRY LOVE
-M-

You and her .
with her the whole world will swirl in your head.
A smooth, strawberry, strongly feminine
drink made only from liqueurs.
Try it, and you certainly will not regret it !

Strawberry Love

Ingredients:

Preparation time: 15 min
Serves: 1

- 40 ml of coconut liqueur
- 40 ml of coco or chocolate liqueur
- 40 ml of cream liqueur
- 40 ml of condensed milk
- 6 strawberries

Instructions:

Place all ingredients in a blender and blend until combined. Pour into a glass and serve.

CRAZY FROG
-S-

It can be made in a few moments
and you only need 2 alcohols –
Rum and Blue Curacao liqueur, nothing will happen if
you replace the liqueur with syrup.
Add pineapple juice and some tonic,
which will give the drink a hint of bitterness.

Crazy Frog

Preparation
time: 10 min
Serves: 1

Ingredients:

- 50 ml of rum
- 20 ml of Blue Curacao liqueur
- 100ml of pineapple juice
- tonic to top-up

Instructions:

Mix the first three ingredients
in a shaker with ice cubes.
Pour into a glass over ice and
top with tonic.

★ ★ ★ ★ ★

11

WHITE LADY
-S-

White Lady is a very simple drink, although to make it we
need a bitter orange liqueur.
Any Triple Sec liqueur will do. The drink is quite strong,
but gin lovers will certainly enjoy it.

White Lady

Preparation
time: 10 min
Serves: 1

Ingredients:

- 40ml of gin
- 30ml of triple sec liqueur
- 20ml of lemon juice
- ice cubes
- Lemon peel
  for garnish

Instructions:

Shake all ingredients in a
shaker with ice cubes.
Strain into a cocktail
glass, garnish with lemon
peel.

GREEN LIGHT
-S-

A tequila drink, sweet and exotic –
just right for summer.

One of the easiest drinks to make, good for parties
because you can make it quickly.
You can make it without a shaker too – just stir with
a straw in a glass if you don't have a shaker at hand.
Blue Curacao syrup can be replaced by liqueur if
you want a stronger drink.
The color of the drink is beautiful, the taste is great –
now go and try it !

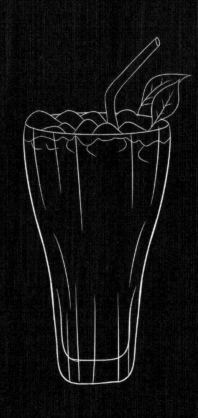

Green Light

Preparation
time: 10 min
Serves: 1

Ingredients:

- 60 ml of tequila silver
- 80 ml of orange juice
- 80 ml of pineapple juice
- 15 ml of Blue Curacao syrup
- ice cubes

Instructions:

Place ingredients in a shaker
and mix with 2-3 ice cubes.
Pour into a tall glass over ice
and serve.

MAI TAI
-S-

Drink in which the main role is played by rum – light,
and dark. Added to it are exotic flavors of
pineapple and almonds.
Mai Tai is a drink known and enjoyed in many
places around the world. You can find it in bar
menus almost everywhere.
It is worth trying Mai Tai at least once, especially if
you likes Rum.

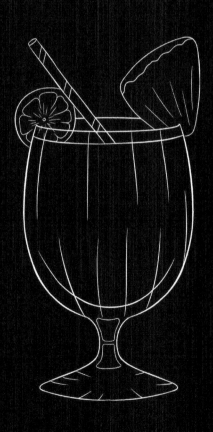

La Isla Bonita

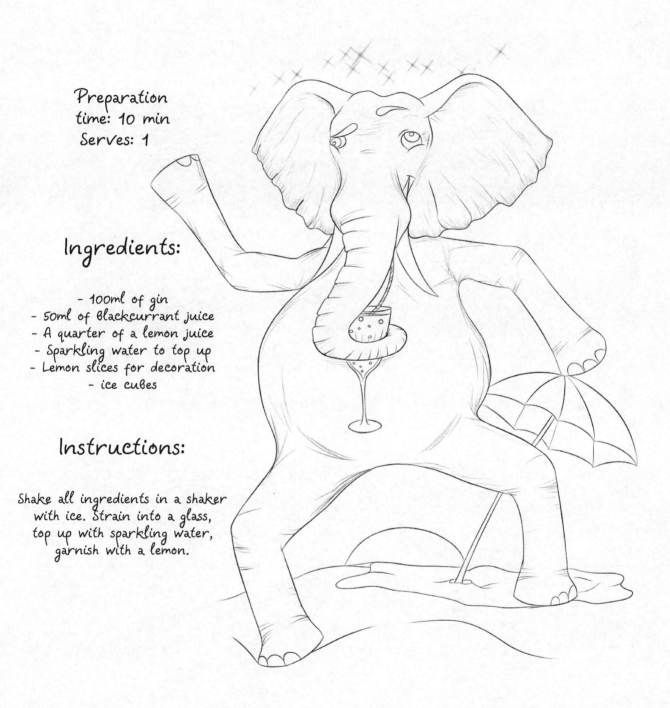

Preparation
time: 10 min
Serves: 1

Ingredients:

- 100ml of gin
- 50ml of blackcurrant juice
- A quarter of a lemon juice
- Sparkling water to top up
- Lemon slices for decoration
- ice cubes

Instructions:

Shake all ingredients in a shaker
with ice. Strain into a glass,
top up with sparkling water,
garnish with a lemon.

★ ★ ★ ★ ★

WATERMELON DAIQUIRI
-S-

Daiquiri is undoubtedly the perfect base
for drink experiments.
All you need to do to the basic recipe is add a little bit
of bartender fruit syrup and the drink takes on a whole
new character. I think Italian bartender syrups are
perfect for this recipe, they are usually thick and have a
very intense fruit flavor.

Watermelon Daiquiri

Ingredients:

- 40 ml of white rum
- 20 ml of lime juice
- 10 ml of watermelon syrup
- ice cubes
- melon or watermelon for garnish

Preparation time: 10 min
Serves: 1

Instructions:

Shake all ingredients in a shaker with ice cubes, then strain into a cocktail glass. Garnish with a slice of melon or watermelon.

AUGUSTUS
-S-

Drink for those who like herbal flavors – the main
role is played here by the liqueur whose taste you
can smell without a doubt.
I recommend a German liqueur in a characteristic
green bottle with a picture of a deer. Its worth
trying it at least once in your life. Some people love
it, others hate the unique herbal taste.
This drink is a way to dampen the particular flavor
of the liqueur – a drink in sweeter climates.

Augustus

Preparation
time: 10 min
Serves: 1

Ingredients:

- 40 ml of vodka
- 30 ml of herb & spice
  liqueur
- 15 ml of grenadine
- A quarter of a lime juice
- crushed ice
- lemon and lime soda to
  top-up

Instructions:

Shake vodka, liqueur,
grenadine, and lime juice in a
shaker.
Pour into a glass over
crushed ice, top up with citrus
flavored soda
(about 50-100 ml).

☆ ☆ ☆ ☆ ☆

23

CRAZY DANCING
-S-

A drink that will charm every woman.
It is composed of simple ingredients that blend into a
beautiful red color,
combined with rum, it's reminiscent of a hot summer.
And its name is Crazy Dancing – you will surely have
a good time dancing after this drink :)

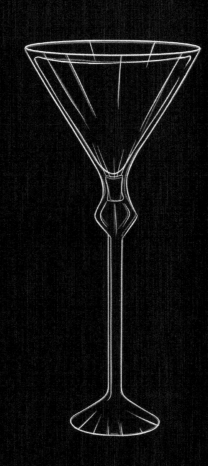

Crazy Dancing

Preparation
time: 10 min
Serves: 1

Ingredients

- 50 ml of white rum
- 50 ml of lemon juice
- 30 ml of grenadine
- lemon-lime soda to top-up
- A slice of lemon to garnish
- ice cubes

Instructions:

Mix the first three
ingredients in a shaker
with ice. Strain into a
glass over ice,
Fill with lemon-lime soda
and put half a slice of
lemon in the middle.

PLANTER'S PUNCH
-S-

A mix of perfect drink for people who love sour flavors with a hint of sweetness.
It is a gently warming drink because there is only rum. It will positively surprise not one palate :)
A small fun fact - 1 dash is 8-10 drops. It is a measure used to measure Bitters.

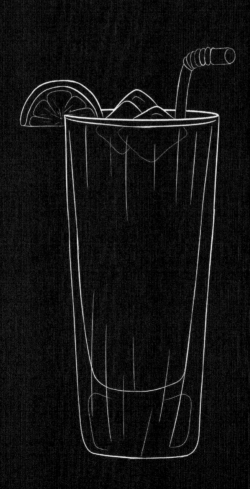

Planter's Punch

Ingredients:

- 45 ml of dark rum
- 35 ml of orange juice
- 35 ml of pineapple juice
- 20 ml of lemon juice
- 10 ml of sugar syrup
- 10 ml of grenadine syrup
- 4 dashes of Bitters
- ice cubes
- Pineapple slice for garnish

Preparation
time: 15 min
Serves: 1

Instructions:

In a shaker with ice cubes,
shake all ingredients.
Strain into a tall ice cube
glass and garnish with
pineapple.

FROM DUSK TILL DAWN
-S-

A layered colorful drink with a herbal flair.

Drink From Dusk Till Dawn looks complicated
but in fact, there are simple ingredients
- only liquor and vodka, juice, and syrup.
The orange flavor of the Blue Curacao syrup
matches the herbal liqueur, so despite the unusual
color, the drink is quite pleasant in taste.

From Dusk Till Dawn

Preparation
time: 15 min
Serves: 1

Ingredients:

- 20 ml of Blue Curacao syrup
- 150 ml of grapefruit juice
- 50 ml of vodka
- 30 ml of herb & spice liqueur
- ice cubes

Instructions:

In a shaker, mix grapefruit
juice and vodka. Pour into a
tall glass over ice,
add Blue Curacao syrup, which
should fall to the bottom.
Gently pour the herbal liqueur
on top.

29

HONEY CAKE WHITE RUSSIAN
-S-

A variation on one of the classics The White Russian.
If you want to mix things up, even more,
try replacing the regular vodka with a flavored one,
such as hazelnut. The gingerbread flavor is something
else, it will surely surprise you :)

Honey Cake White Russian

Preparation
time: 15 min
Serves: 1

Ingredients:

- 40 ml of vodka
- 20 ml of coffee liqueur
- 30 ml of condensed
  unsweetened milk
- teaspoon gingerbread
  spice
- ice cubes
- Cinnamon stick for
  decoration

Instructions:

Pour milk into a shaker with ice cubes and add
gingerbread spice. Shake to combine ingredients.
Pour vodka, coffee liqueur, and the contents of the shaker
into an ice cube glass.

☆ ☆ ☆ ☆ ☆

SWEET STRAWBERRY WHISKY
-S-

A whiskey drink with a sweet note, with lots of
crushed ice and a strawberry garnish.
Just right for a slow sip on warmer days.
Drinks with crushed ice are mostly drank in summer,
but you can make them at home any time of year.
It's good to have an ice crusher on hand, because it
makes things easier, although you can also manage
without one
(for example, by wrapping ice in a cloth and
pounding with a meat tenderizer).

Sweet Strawberry Whisky

Preparation
time: 15 min
Serves: 1

Ingredients:

- 50 ml of whisky
- 30 ml of strawberry syrup
- Sparkling water
- 3 strawberries
- Lemon quarter
- crushed ice

Instructions:

Pour crushed ice into a glass
(up to half of the glass),
Pour whisky and syrup,
previously mixed in a
shaker.
Add the strawberries cut in
quarters, the lemon, fill up
with crushed ice and add
sparkling water (a splash,
not too much). And done :)

TENNESSEE CHERRY
-S-

This time we're going to delve into the combination of flavorful cherry liqueur and equally flavorful Tennessee whiskey.

Did you know that Tennessee whiskey is so popular that there are even songs sung about it? Surely everyone knows the distinctive label, which has also become an inspiration for the creation of T-shirts, posters, and various gadgets.

Tennessee Cherry

Preparation time: 15 min
Serves: 1

Ingredients:

- 50 ml of whiskey
- 30 ml of cherry liqueur
- 20ml of sugar syrup
- Sparkling water
- quarter of lemon

Instructions:

Pour crushed ice into a glass, halfway up. Mix whiskey in a shaker with liqueur and sugar syrup
(if you prefer less sweet flavors, you can omit the sugar syrup). Pour contents of shaker over crushed ice, Stir with a spoon, add the rest of the crushed ice, lemon and top up with sparkling water. Enjoy the taste :)

TROPICAL HEAT
-S-

Delicious taste, beautiful and impressive appearance
of this tri-colored drink - satisfaction guaranteed !

This drink is sure to please you. It seems to be very
difficult, but to make the Tropical Heat
we only need four ingredients and those are the ones
that every fan of drinks certainly has in their alcohol
cupboard.

Tropical Heat

Ingredients:

- 20 ml of grenadine
- 50 ml of rum
- 50 ml of Blue Curacao liqueur (cannot be syrup)
- approx. 300 ml orange juice (depending on the size of the glass)
- Ice cubes

Instructions:

Put lots of ice cubes in a glass. Pour the grenadine into the bottom. Then gently pour in the orange juice, spoon by spoon.
Mix Rum and Blue Curacao in a shaker (but no ice cubes!). Pour the contents of the shaker into the glass, also gently, a spoonful at a time. The layers should separate without much problem.

Preparation time: 15 min
Serves: 1

SIX CYCLE
-S-

Beautiful drink - one of the prettiest, but most
difficult to make in the whole book,
after so much practice, I'm sure you can handle it :)

I will tell you a secret. Do you know what is on the
other side of the rainbow? A cauldron.
In this cauldron- on Six Cycle. More precious than
gold. It tastes as fabulous as it looks!

Six Cycle

Preparation time: 15 min
Serves: 1

Ingredients:

- 90 ml of white rum
- 40 ml of cherry liqueur
- 150 ml of orange juice
- approx. 1 tbsp grenadine
- 20 ml of Blue Curacao liqueur
- 150 ml sparkling wine/champagne

Instructions:

In a shaker (no ice cubes - this is important), shake rum, maraschino liqueur, and orange juice. Pour into a glass.
Add grenadine, which will settle on the bottom. In a clean glass or pitcher, mix the Blue Curacao liqueur and sparkling wine - pour both ingredients into the glass and stir gently with a spoon.
Pour the blue-tinged champagne gently into the glass - it's best to do this with the spoon turned upside down, against the wall of the glass so that the layers form and the drinks do not mix together.
You can use orange, lemon, carambola, and cocktail cherry to garnish.

COCONUT SUNRISE
-W-

This is a drink from a series that I like the most – you do not need a shaker here, you can do several pieces at once, pouring alcohol and juices into the glass. During a party, when we need to prepare drinks for several guests at the same time – such recipes work best. Besides the coconut-rum liqueur, you can add here either vodka or tequila – as you like. This drink will spice up your party in a few moments :)

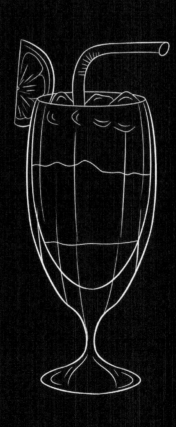

Coconut Sunrise

Preparation
time: 10 min
Serves: 1

Ingredients:

- 40 ml of vodka
- 30 ml coconut-rum
  liqueur
- Orange juice to top-up
- A few drops of grenadine

Instructions:

Pour the vodka and liqueur
into an ice cube glass, top
up with orange juice and
finally add the grenadine.
Optionally, you can add a
teaspoon of lemon juice if
you prefer less sweet
drinks.

⭐ ⭐ ⭐ ⭐ ⭐

BLUE LAGOON
-W-

Simple, you don't need many ingredients for it, so it will
work great at any party
Blue Lagoon will certainly taste good to all those who
like gin but not necessarily bitter gin and tonic, but
rather sweet compositions.
This drink is exactly like that - sweet with only a slight
bitter aftertaste all thanks to blue curacao liqueur.
It will take you literally seconds to make.

Blue Lagoon

Preparation
time: 10 min
Serves: 1

Ingredients:

- 40 ml of vodka
- 20 ml of Blue curacao
  liqueur
- lemon-lime soda
  to top-up
- ice cubes
- Orange slice for
  decoration

Instructions:

Put ice cubes in a tall
glass, pour in vodka and
liquor one at a time, top
off with lemon-lime soda.

MOJITO WITH RASPBERRIES
-W-

A sensational mojito with the addition of fresh
raspberries. It will taste equally good in the virgin
version, that is without alcohol.
I know that there are a lot of mojito maniacs and
they will certainly like this drink the most.
Anyway, I recommend it to everyone for summer
days - you can prepare it in a non-alcoholic version
in the morning and even give it to children.
In the evening it will be great with rum,
holiday and refreshing.
Just like a mojito with raspberries you can make a
mojito with other fruits :)

Mojito With Raspberries

Preparation time: 10 min
Serves: 1

Ingredients:

- 40 ml of rum
- half of a lime + slice for decoration
- 2 teaspoons of brown sugar
- 8-10 mint leaves
- a handful of raspberries + 2-3 for decoration
- a few ice cubes or crushed ice
- Sparkling water to top-up

Instructions:

In a glass put a lime cut in eights, sugar, raspberries, mint. We knead everything quite hard, to let the fruit juice out. Add rum, mix, add ice cubes and finally top up with sparkling water.
Add a slice of lime and raspberries for decoration. Serve with a thick straw.

BLACKCURRANT GINITO
-W-

This drink is simply brilliant!

The combination of currant vodka, gin, lime juice, and sugar… you can immediately sense that it must be something delicious!
The advantage of this drink is not only its taste but also its appearance – the photo does not show it well, but the color is fantastic. This is a drink that you can drink all evening and never get bored.

Blackcurrant Gintio

Preparation
time: 15 min
Serves: 1

Ingredients:

- 30ml of gin
- 30ml of currant vodka
- half a lime
- 2 teaspoons brown sugar
- tonic to top-up
- ice cubes

Instructions:

Cut the lime into quarters, and cut each lime into 3 more pieces. Put into a glass, add sugar, and muddle. When the lime has released a lot of juice, add the spirits and stir - either with a stirrer or a bartender's spoon. Add ice cubes and top up with tonic.

★ ★ ★ ★ ★

BITTERS

This is probably the trendiest ingredient in cocktails lately. There are more and more bitters on the market, but the best looking cocktail is one based on bartender's own bitters.
Bitters are nothing but bitter drops.
The bitterness is needed for the drink to have the right balance.

KAMIKAZE IN 5 COLORS

This classic is probably already known to everyone, although not necessarily in such colour variations :) KAMIKAZE – these are delicious shots that can be prepared in the blink of an eye and in larger quantities.
They are perfect for a party, and these 5 colours are certainly something that will appeal to all and provides an unforgettable experience :)

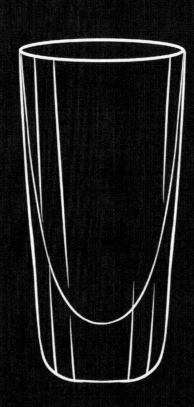

Kanikaze In 5 Colors

Ingredients:

BLUE

- 40 ml of vodka
- 40 ml of Blue Curacao liqueur
- 40 ml of lemon juice

GREEN

- 40 ml of vodka
- 40 ml of mint liqueur
- 40 ml of lemon juice

YELLOW

- 40 ml of vodka
- 40 ml of flavoured vodka - passion fruit
- 40 ml of lemon juice

RED

- 40 ml of vodka
- 40 ml of watermelon flavoured vodka
- 40 ml of lemon juice

DARK GREEN

- 40 ml of black vodka
- 40 ml of Blue Curacao liqueur
- 40 ml of lemon juice

Preparation time: 3 min
Serves: 3

Instructions:

Simple and quickly, just shake the ingredients in a shaker and pour into glasses. Each recipe gives us 3 shots if the glasses have 40ml of. Do it!

⭐ ⭐ ⭐ ⭐ ⭐

COLORFUL MAD DOGS

After the colourful Kamikaze, it's time for the colourful
Mad Dogs. Coloured rabid dogs are perfect as
welcome shots at a house party.
I also encourage you to try the "very angry dog" (Pour
1/2 cherry liqueur into a glass, and then gently, a
tablespoon at a time, pour in the 1/2 spirit.
Add a few drops of Tabasco. Drink at once.
Very angry dog is rather not a shot to drink in larger
quantities since it is very strong,
so, I recommend it only to brave drink lovers :)

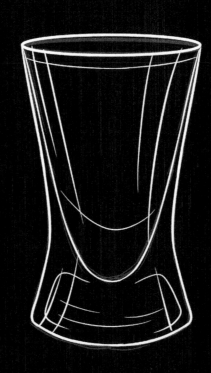

Colorful Mad Dogs

Ingredients:

- vodka
- tabasco
- syrups in different colours: raspberry, Black currant, Blue curacao, peach, orange, ginger, mint, etc.

Instructions:

Pour the vodka into the glass and gently add the syrup - so, So that in 1/3 of the glass there is syrup and in 2/3 vodka. At the end add 1-2 drops of Tabasco.

Preparation time: 5 min
Serves: 1

⭐⭐⭐⭐⭐

SHOT
AMERICAN FLAG

A colourful, three - layer shot in the colours of the
flag, and not just one :)
This shot looks very impressive and
is quite easy to make.
The ingredients are quite different in density, and it's
easy to pour them to make three layers. The shot is
called American Flag, although it's more associated
with the French flag, only upside down.

Shot American Flag

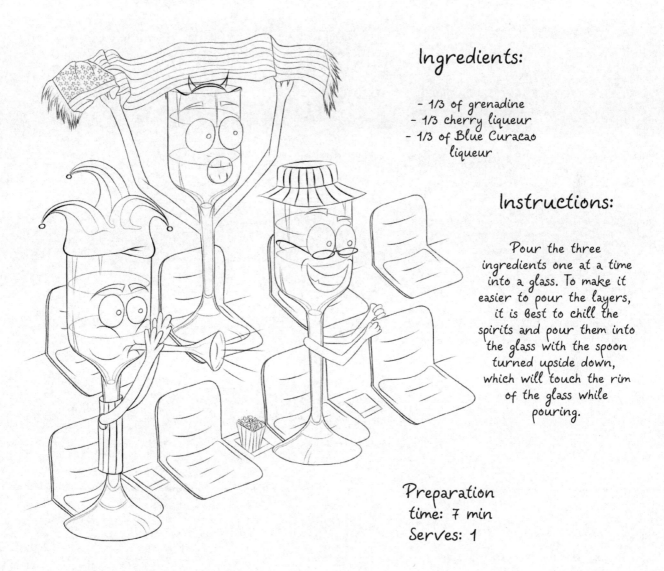

Ingredients:

- 1/3 of grenadine
- 1/3 cherry liqueur
- 1/3 of Blue Curacao
  liqueur

Instructions:

Pour the three ingredients one at a time into a glass. To make it easier to pour the layers, it is best to chill the spirits and pour them into the glass with the spoon turned upside down, which will touch the rim of the glass while pouring.

Preparation
time: 7 min
Serves: 1

⭐ ⭐ ⭐ ⭐ ⭐

SHOT RIO

Good even very good composition of mint and
orange - shot Rio.
These three colours - blue, green, and yellow, yes, this
time a reference to the Brazilian climate.
What to say.... Just try it and for sure your taste
buds will not regret it :)

Shot Rio

Preparation
time: 5 min
Serves: 1

Ingredients:

- 1/5 of Blue Curacao
  syrup
- 2/5 of mint liqueur
- 2/5 of orange vodka

Instructions:

Pour the ingredients into the glass in
the order given, for the second and
third it is best to use a pouring glass
and pour the spirits gently by spoonful
to make it easier to create layers.

SHOT
CREAM STRAWBERRIES

Sweet, easy to make, the taste is simply
out of this world.
This is one of those layered shots that comes out
without a problem – the difference in density between
the strawberry liqueur and vodka is very large, so the
layers separate nicely. Anyway, instead of liqueur, you
can use strawberry syrup – maybe a little less,
because then the shot would be too sweet, but the
layers will also fall into place.
Adding a few drops of milk or coffee creamer is a
nice finishing touch to this drink.

Shot Cream Strawberries

Preparation time: 5 min
Serves: 1

Ingredients:

- 1/2 of strawberry liqueur
- 1/2 vodka
- A few drops of milk or coffee cream

Instructions:

Pour the strawberry liqueur into a glass and then gently pour in the vodka, preferably with an upturned spoon to form layers. Finally, using a straw or a spoon, add a few drops of milk or coffee cream.

☆☆☆☆☆

SHOT
PERSISTENT PARTYGOER

A shot with a bizarre appearance and
an even more intriguing taste.
It's not difficult, because the density of the alcohols used
varies enough that it's easy to get a layered effect.
And the addition of grenadine at the end makes
everything mix in an interesting way.
Interesting fact - every time you use a different cream
liqueur the layers should look different,
because they can have different density - peach on the
bottom, cream in the middle, herbs on top.
Worth a try :)

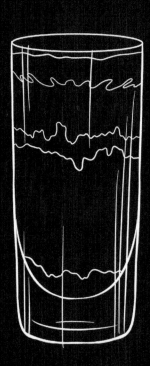

Shot Persistent Partygoer

Preparation
time: 7 min
Serves: 1

Ingredients:

- 1/2 of cream liqueur
- 1/4 of peach liqueur
- 1/4 of herb & spice liqueur
- a few drops of grenadine

Instructions:

Pour the cream liqueur into a long glass. Then gently pour in peach liqueur by the spoonful and in third order.
- herbal and spice liqueur. At the very end add a few drops of grenadine, it is best to pour it earlier on a spoon or into a bottle stopper. The layers should form without much trouble.

CLOUD SHOT

Cloud – an intriguing shot that looks fabulous in a glass!

Interesting fact: this drink has different names. I am most convinced by Cloud because of its appearance, the drink is sometimes called the Seed of the Bartender or the Seed of the Bull.

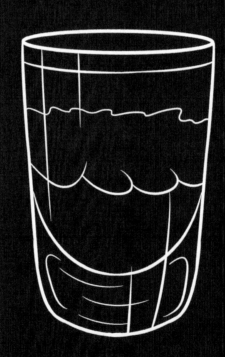

Cloud Shot

Preparation
time: 5 min
Serves: 1

Ingredients:

- 1/2 glass of vodka
- 1/2 glass of peach
  liqueur
- a few drops of
  condensed milk

Instructions:

Pour the peach liqueur
into the glass, then
gently, down the wall
pour the vodka to form
the top layer.
Using a straw, scoop
some condensed milk,
which you then pour
into the glass.
The milk forms a cloud-
like middle layer.

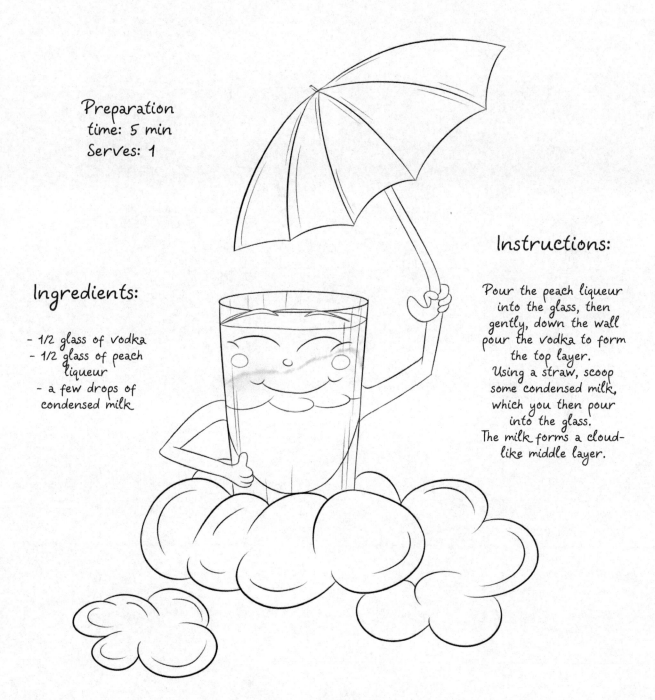

SHOT
MONKEY BRAIN

A Monkey Brain shot that makes an
electrifying visual impression.

Monkey Brain is a shot that looks really impressive but
making it is really easy. The secret is that just like other
layered shots - to make Monkey Brain you need two
alcohols of different densities. In this case, it's a peach
liqueur and cream liqueur, which are poured one by
one into the glass, and a few drops of grenadine. The
effect is amazing, that's why Monkey Brain is perfect
for a Halloween party.

Shot Monkey Brain

Preparation
time: 5 min
Serves: 1

Ingredients:

- 1/2 glass of peach liqueur
- 1/2 glass of cream liqueur
- a few drops of grenadine

Instructions:

Pour the peach liqueur into the glass, then gently, pour the cream liqueur down the sides of the glass, which will form a second layer. Finally, add a few drops of grenadine.

SHOT
STRAWBERRY CAKE

Strawberry shot to be prepared in several servings at once – just right for girls' gatherings.

Not too strong, sweet, with a fruity taste, and additionally, with cream liqueur. I don't think I know a woman who wouldn't like this liqueur. And if you combine the liqueur with the taste of strawberries and milk – how can it not come out tasting amazing.

Shot Strawberry Cake

Preparation
time: 5 min
Serves: 3

Ingredients:

- 1/3 of strawberry liqueur
- 1/3 of cream liqueur
- 1/3 of condensed milk

Instructions:

Pour all three ingredients into a shaker and
shake vigorously to combine.
I suggest you pour a glass of each ingredient
and then you'll get a serving for 3 glasses.
For an extra visual effect use a crust of
cake sprinkles and strawberry syrup.

SHOT
ALIEN BRAIN HEMORRHAGE

A bone-chilling shot - this is something you must try !
The cream combined with the peach liqueur behaves
unusually - it congeals, to form interesting shapes.
With the combination of these two spirits, we get a
shot, that looks and feels like the real thing, and that's
what it's called. It sounds terrible and looks terrible,
but it doesn't taste too bad.

Shot Alien Brain Hemorrhage

Preparation
time: 3 min
Serves: 1

Ingredients:

- 1/2 glass of peach liqueur
- 1/4 glass of cream liqueur
- a few drops of Blue Curacao
- a few drops of grenadine

Instructions:

Pour the ingredients one by one into the glass in the order listed. This time the speed is not important, there will be no layers. We do not use a spoon and thanks to this the effect will be much more interesting, just pour the individual ingredients.

CRUSTA

Glass decoration, used mainly with alcoholic beverages.
It is made by wetting the edge of the glass (e.g. with fruit syrup),
and then touching the edge of the glass with sugar spilled on the plate or
sugar spilled on a plate and then touching the rim of the glass with a sprinkle of sugar or other powdery substance that can decorate our drink or shot.

COLOR TEST

I hope you liked the coloring book, i put all my effort into it.

I would be delighted if you share your opinion about it on Amazon, it will help to expand my profile and encourage me to create more.

THANK YOU

Printed in Great Britain
by Amazon

83808206R00045